# urban tails

# inside the hidden world of alley cats

photography by Knox

text by Sara Neeley

New World Library
Novato, California

New World Library
14 Pamaron Way
Novato, California 94949

Text design by Mary Ann Casler

Library of Congress Cataloging-in-Publication Data
Knox.
Urban tails: inside the hidden world of alley cats / photos by Knox ; text by Sara Neeley.
     p.   cm.
ISBN-13: 978-1-57731-560-5 (hardcover : alk. paper)
1.  Feral cats—Georgia—Atlanta. 2.  Feral cats—Georgia—Atlanta—Pictorial works.
I. Neeley, Sara. II. Title.
SF450.K662 2006
636.8'09758'231022—dc22                          2006009097

First printing, October 2006
ISBN-10: 1-57731-560-X
ISBN-13: 978-1-57731-560-5

Printed in Hong Kong
Distributed by Publishers Group West

10  9  8  7  6  5  4  3  2  1

We dedicate this book in loving memory of Dr. Bruce Neeley,

a physician to humans, whose love of and respect for all life

continues to serve as a lighthouse for us.

# ACKNOWLEDGMENTS

**KNOX:** Special thanks to HP, Sam and Harriet, Bob McCullough, my attorney and friend Bob Donnelly, Sara Neeley, Amelia Kinkade, Jason Gardner and Mary Ann Casler and everyone at NWL, Lukas and Dekker Black, NYC, Miguel Perales, DVM, and Twelve Incredible Steps to a brand new life.

**SARA:** Many people influenced us as we worked on this book. Our personal veterinarians at Buckhead Animal Clinic and Alpharetta Animal Hospital gave us heavily discounted services as we sought to neuter and care for our stray and feral cats and kittens.

Nancy Peterson of the Humane Society of the United States has been a friend, supporter,

Our friends Diane Leigh and Marilee Geyer and their book *One at a Time: A Week in an American Animal Shelter* absolutely convinced us that animal shelters are not the answer.

Unknowingly, cartoonist Patrick McDonnell, creator of *Mutts*, was an initial inspiration with his humorous, gentle portrayal of animal life and the interdependence of all life-forms that share this planet.

Most important, I thank my cat friends. Two must be mentioned, as they influence the heart of everything I do: Doc, an "old soul," and Mel, absolutely the gentlest cat I've ever had the joy of loving. Each cat has brought untold joy into my life and the lives of my family and friends.

# FOREWORD

I love cats — big and small, long- and short-haired, elegant and scruffy, young and old — and I hope you do, too. I have been fortunate to share my life with many. They have all had one trait in common: homelessness.

Buddy was five months old when he was found wandering in a busy parking lot. Daisy was at least one year old when she was left behind on the street when her family moved. Stu was five months old when he was found unconscious on the side of the road. And Monty, the most decrepit cat I'd ever met, was estimated to be at least thirteen when he was found crouching under a car. Buddy and Stu lived to be seventeen, Daisy nineteen, and Monty, well, I had him for fourteen years. For the most part, we shared wonderful years together. Of course, no relationship is perfect and ours had their challenges. I miss them still. Although I couldn't adopt all the homeless cats who came to the clinic where I worked as a veterinary technician, my co-workers, family, and friends were willing to provide loving homes for the others.

I now share my home with my sister and our two sister cats, Zubi and Luna. They, along

feline rescue in Merrifield, Virginia, the Feline Foundation of Greater Washington. Someone fed them, and thus they were spared the pain of hunger. They weren't spared the risk of cars, poisons, inclement weather, disease, pregnancy, and possible death. It breaks my heart to imagine what would have become of my cats, and many others, had they not found loving homes.

This is a beautiful book about the not-so-beautiful plight of homeless cats who are left to fend for themselves. I hope you are touched as much as I am by the book's images and words and that you will help homeless cats where you live — by providing a loving home if the cats are tame or can be tamed and by learning about Trap-Neuter-Return (TNR) programs if the cats are feral. It is only through our combined efforts that, one precious life at a time, all cats will have the care they deserve.

Nancy Peterson
Feral Cat Program Manager
The Humane Society of the United States
Washington, DC

# INTRODUCTION

**B**ehind office buildings, theaters, restaurants, and shopping malls everywhere live families of stray cats. Similar scenes unfold near any dumpster or source of water. Our parents called them alley cats. "Strays," we mutter, although the correct term is probably "feral." A stray cat is one who has had contact with people at some point in its life and may now be lost, or worse, abandoned. A feral cat has been completely alone and wild since birth. Regardless of what we call them, there are so many strays that we hardly notice their existence. It's not that we ignore them; we rarely even see them. But when we have the courage to look into their eyes, we recognize their hunger and fear as primal instincts that we, too, can have, and it stirs our guilt and anxiety. Although alley cats are certainly not exclusively an urban problem, the focus of our photographs is "city cats." We choose this designation for our cats and kittens, since ours all live in large metropolitan environments.

Like an unfolding drama, our pictures and stories will involve you in the ongoing lives and problems of these little street warriors. You will not be able to overlook either the obstacles they face or the joy they find in living. Approximately 3,500 kittens are born every hour in the United States, compared to only 415 children in the same time period. The problem is, probably only one out of every three of these kittens, or approximately 1,200, ends up in a good home with proper care. The situation worsens for those who remain uncared for. Survival becomes a daily battle for food, shelter safe from predators, freedom from disease, protection from the elements, and defense against human ignorance and cruelty.

And the numbers relentlessly increase. A stray female that remains unspayed and her mate can, in ten years, produce as many as one million kittens. "Incredible!" you say. "How?" you ask. Since we obviously value the impact of pictures, let's look at the offspring of one unspayed female cat and her mate.

- 1st year: 12
- 2nd year: 66
- 3rd year: 382
- 4th year: 2,201
- 5th year: 12,680
- 6th year: 73,041
- 7th year: 420,715
- 8th year: 2,423,316
- 9th year: 13,968,290
- 10th year: 80,399,780

Of course, this chart does not take into account any other females whom the same unneutered male might have impregnated. You begin to get the picture. Ultimately, the exact number of cats resulting over time from a single union varies widely. It's obvious that there are too many mouths to feed. There is no way humans can take care of so many stray or feral cats. In an attempt to help, many people take cats or kittens to the local animal shelter, thinking the shelter will find homes for them. Of course, many of the cats are beyond rehabilitation, either because of health or personality. Since homes are found for so very few, euthanasia awaits most alley cats who find themselves in an animal shelter. This, too, is an unacceptable solution for more than merely emotional or ethical reasons. As with everything else in our world, money is a factor, and euthanasia is expensive. The Humane Society of the United States estimates that animal shelters euthanize three to four million dogs and cats every year. This number includes requests by owners, animals who are too young, sick, injured, or aggressive, as well as adoptable animals for whom no homes can be found. The cost of capturing the cats, holding them, feeding

them, and euthanizing them averages $105 per cat. Obviously, since the alley cats can't pay this tab, the taxpayers must.

However, a very effective method of handling the feral cat overpopulation is a relatively new program that involves trapping, neutering, and returning the cats to their original environment (TNR), followed by management of the cat colony from which the strays originally came. TNR is a volunteer program that originally began in England and gradually spread to the United States. Potential TNR volunteers are already in place; a large number of households feed stray cats, and once they learn about TNR, these people are often eager to take the next step and participate in the program. (And while feeding certainly makes the cats' lives easier in the short term, it ultimately does little, since the colonies continue to grow and spread.)

Unquestionably, sterilization is the most important element of a TNR program, for it is through sterilization that attrition occurs within individual cat colonies. In cities across the United States, virtually all vets will charge discounted rates for the neutering of feral cats. Many vets spend long hours dedicated only to spaying and neutering strays. These same vets will also test cats for disease and vaccinate those that are disease-free prior to neutering them, again for a reduced fee. However, if a volunteer cannot afford testing and shots, they can forgo those expenses; the only essential step is neutering.

Studies verify that dedicated TNR programs can reduce the free-roaming cat population by as much as 50 percent. Finding homes for amenable cats following neutering is often possible. If not, the cat can be returned to its original colony, where volunteers can continue to feed and watch over it. Generally speaking, cats that are part of this managed program frequently become used to human involvement in their lives and go on to live as healthily as their indoor counterparts.

Over the past two years, like the Jane Goodalls of the cat world, we have spent literally hundreds of hours observing, photographing, and playing with "our" city cats. Additionally, we have followed a TNR program of our own, with continuing management for these little creatures. (We overlooked a solitary female in our quest to spay. We include her story as well, for she validates the concern over a single female that remains unspayed.)

Like the human homeless, these street cats struggle for survival right beneath our noses. We are going to introduce you to all of the characters in our cat city. Our stories and photographs seek to paint the true spirits that exist in each of our alley cats. Some pictures and stories will, we hope, make you smile or laugh, for some of these city cats have been taken into loving homes. Others will tug at your heart or disturb you, for not all of the cats and kittens you see are still alive. However, for the majority of our alley cats, the daily routine of survival and reproduction continues. Every photograph and story in this book claims a piece of our hearts. Read and lend it your heart, for these alley cats, who exist on this planet by the same birthright as we do, are here at our mercy.

# A PHOTOGRAPHER'S JOURNEY

I knew she was dying. I saw her paw reaching out to me. . . .

I knew her when she was a kitten. I have known these alley cats for a long time. They live next to my studio. Or I should say, my studio is next to where they live. At first I would see them climbing in the dumpsters, hidden in abandoned cars, behind eighteen-wheelers, or sitting on the roof of the studio. They were just shadows — a tiny head sticking out from a dumpster or a rustling of trash when they ran off as I walked Lukas, my dog.

These shadows and rustlings soon became my friends and neighbors, each christened with his or her gang name: Muncher, Knuckles, Hot Rod, Razor, Donkey, Little Gal. Maybe I relate to them because I always saw myself as an underdog. I've seen litters come and go. I've found some of them homes, but I've also witnessed the deaths of many of my friends to the elements, city coyotes, and human cruelty and prejudice. I've pulled pieces of a friend from the road or parking lot here at the studio and dug graves in the sleet to give a proper burial.

I've cared for my neighbors a long time, and they've cared for me. When the city turned dark and lonely, we shared hours together. Many nights I would sit with my neighbors by a street-light, soaking up the silence and calm — a few heartbeats sharing moments in the night. Each night, the urban setting and emotions wrapped around us. Late at night, even the ones who were unsure of me would come close, as if to say, "I understand that you are here for us, and we, too, are here for you. We need and respect your companionship." Early on, they knew I was their friend, and I feel they somehow realized that they gave me comfort, too — all of us children of a Higher Power, one no better than any other. In my heart, it is an honor to be trusted by them. I am the only human who has ever touched most of them.

This dying mom, christened Spooner, who was now reaching out her weak and feeble paw toward me, had her first litter a few months back. I never had hopes that she would be a good mother since she was always aloof and a little strange. I was wrong. I watched her care for and protect her little ones with love, grace, and dignity. Every evening, there she was, sitting above them on a truck, watching the dark for enemies, along with Muncher and Spitter, two other mothers with litters.

A coyote ate one of her little girls early on, and she never was the same. I saw her fight off four raccoons all by herself so she and her kittens could eat the food I put out. I was there the night her mate, a strong, handsome male named Razor, was torn apart by a coyote as he fought hard to protect his litter. I couldn't save him in time, and the screams were deafening. Spooner moaned for hours afterward as she and I searched for him. She would look under dumpsters and cars, all the time turning around to see if I was behind her, helping in the search but also keeping watch over her kittens. Her little kittens lay huddled together, frightened at the screams. The death in the air felt heavy and profound.

But something has happened that never entered my mind. Spooner, the once strong, proud mother, the lioness at heart, is now lying under a truck, wheezing. She's nothing but skin and bones, her face incredibly swollen, distorted out of proportion, her eyes swollen shut. Teenage kittens from other litters lie close by, huddled alongside her, their necks and faces also mysteriously swollen. They're all hacking and lethargic.

Other adults from the alley have joined the huddle. I can now see that none of my friends has escaped this strange illness. Tomorrow I will take my sick friends to the vet to see if they have to be put to sleep. Many little kittens, once playful with each other and their mothers, intertwined with other kittens from other moms, will now be missed and replaced with my solitude. More than a dozen street cats are sick, maybe more: The Nun, Peeping Tom,

Face, Queenie, Possum, Nemesis, and so on. It will be painfully quiet by my door.

The ones who survived have all been spayed and neutered. We feed all of them daily and give them clean water. The ones who survived are now my long-standing friends. As I step out of my studio to walk Lukas, out of the bushes and from behind trucks come Nemesis, Little Gal, Tiny, Muncher, and now Pooch and Spooks, two new editions, to greet me. Pooch, a lone survivor of a litter a skinny little mom dropped off here as she went off to die, comes and goes. Frankie, Spitter, Shakes, and Lucy have recently died. Turk, Hot Rod, and Harvey have all been adopted by humans.

This book is for all who reach out to help suffering animals. Thousands feed, build homes for, and capture, spay, and neuter alley cats all around the world. They do it from their hearts, and it is not easy work. It is emotional, expensive, and time consuming.

It's an honor that animals have let us into their world — especially those who have suffered at human hands yet have learned over time to trust us. The alley cat problem is not a cat problem, but a human one.

We are well aware that our book does not portray the full picture of what alley cats endure. Who would buy a book that accurately showed the suffering they go through? It is my hope that our book offers one perspective on the plight of these little street warriors — a lens showing that the lives around us, which we barely notice, do matter. It is the intent of this book to show that alley cats have emotions similar to ours. They get sick, they love and protect their young, they play, and sadly, they too, fall prey to humanity's dark side. I hope this book inspires you to get involved any way you can. Spaying and neutering is a beginning.

Urban Tails

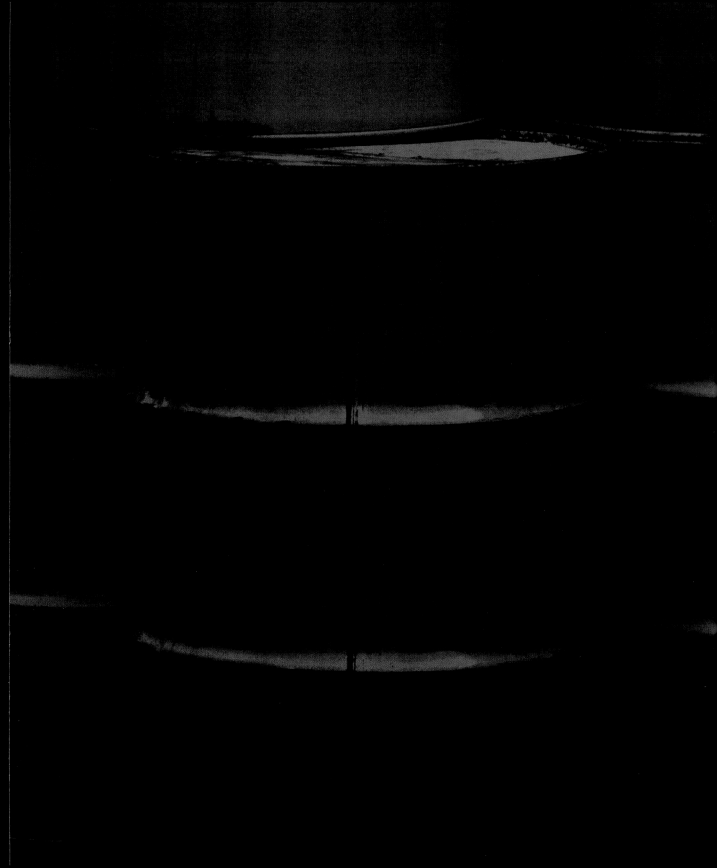

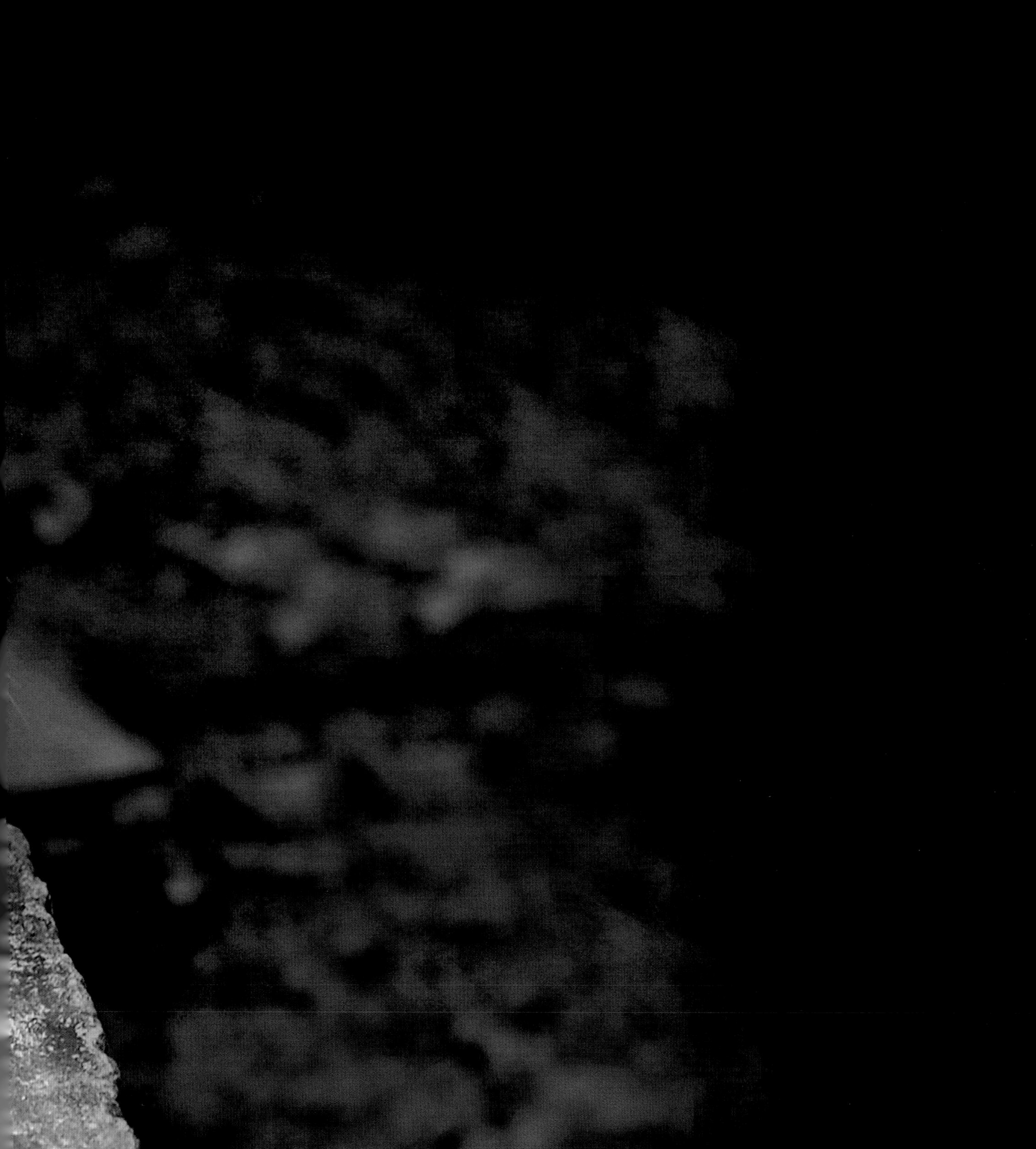

# NEMESIS

With one look at this imposing orange-and-white male, we figured this cat would be any opponent's doom. Thus the name "Nemesis." In temperament, however, he's quite different, even introverted. He's always by himself, a loner. If he were a person, we envision him walking down the city street at 2 AM, head tucked, hands stuffed in his jeans pockets. Nemesis never laughs or smiles; life for him is serious.

Nemesis always approaches with his ears pitched forward, and he is never the first to look away from other cats or people. Most cats quickly realize that deferring, not fighting, is the smarter course of action.

Nemesis is a wanderer. We have noticed him peering from behind bushes that line the front of a nearby bank or searching for rodents around the dumpster in back of the gas station. Remarkably, he knows his name. Whenever we see him in an out-of-the-way spot, we speak to him. He stops and studies us, often for minutes, with clear recognition in his eyes. He seems to be telling us that he will see us again, the next time his walkabout brings him into our territory.

When Nemesis appears in our alley, we know it is for one of two reasons — either he's hungry or in search of a mate. When he's hungry, he looks it. His coat is ragged and dirty; he's clearly lost weight.

course, when he is looking for a mate, he is clearly on the prowl. Females beware! One evening he limped into our alley, clearly hurt; he didn't even make it to the food bowl. We were fairly certain that he had been in a fight; we wondered what his opponent must look like. When we put food out, he managed to hobble to the bowl. We gave him his own special bowl of food, and he did not even shy away. He stayed for three days, eating and sleeping in the sun. On the third morning, he stood up, stretched, ate with gusto, and left.

Over time, Nemesis has come to trust Knox. He will sit just inches from Knox while he eats and will occasionally condescend to let Knox scratch his head. Regardless of how many cans of food I bring him or how much I coo to him, his attitude toward me remains the same: "Not another inch, lady!"

Nemesis continues as the patriarch of our cat community. Because of his inimitable disposition and trademark eyes, it is a special day when Nemesis appears. We are thrilled he continues to survive. We laugh to see his harem faithfully flock to his paw prints when he shows up, and we delight that he deigns to tolerate other cats and us long enough to gulp mouthfuls of food set out for him. As humans so often do, we tend to think that he is less lonely and better off when he is around us.

# KAT

A true rebirth, one of a cat's fabled nine lives, occurred right before our eyes. The proverbial underdog, Kat was a lovely calico, with large, vivid splashes of orange, black, and brown against a white background. Only a bad left eye and a broken tail, probably the results of fights in her younger days, marred her beauty. The rumor was that Kat had lived in the alley that runs behind the office buildings for many years, seeking shelter under parked trucks and cars or under the few bushes on the tiny landscaped plot in front of the back office. Early on, she acquired a Protector, a man who worked in one of the offices. He fed her daily and even spayed and rereleased her. He observed that the other cats chased her from her food, for she was shy and reticent by nature. Again, his caring instincts surfaced and he built her a house and placed it in the alley against the building. Kat's house was the envy of all. Although she had no doorman, she did have an entry hidden and secure from the local raccoons and other predators. One complete side was Plexiglas, from which she could view the goings-on of the outside world while propped up on her many cushions. It even had a shingled roof to keep her dry. She dined outside her front door.

After several years, the Protector lost his job and left Kat. Even though he left her house and continued to come on weekends to bring her food, her life just wasn't the same. She grieved and would disappear for days at a time. We sought to fill the void for Kat by taking over daily feedings, back rubs, and talks. She was such a sweet, personable girl that she quickly became our favorite cat. We worried when we did not see her, but she always returned just when we were convinced that she had met with misfortune.

For some reason, the last litter of kittens born that summer accepted Kat and seemed not only to tolerate but also to enjoy her as part of the group. Their parents, however, refused to extend their hospitality. After dinner, the adult cats made it clear that Kat should retire to her sleeping quarters under the hood of an eighteen-wheeler parked in the alley. (For reasons known only to Kat, she preferred the truck to her home.) With her usual quiet acceptance and grace, Kat would hop up on the wheelbase to perform her nightly cleaning. She would remain for some time, simply watching the activity among the other cats and kittens. Eventually, she would work her way up through the bottom of the cab to sleep next to the motor. Her life remained solitary and lonely.

Eventually, new, less cat-friendly ownership moved into the Protector's former office. They called the Protector and issued and ultimatum: do something with Kat or they would! When Kat disappeared one weekend and did not return, we were inconsolable. What had happened to Kat? Had she run away? Had she been hurt, or worse, killed?

Finally, it was confirmed that the Protector had come to her rescue! Now, she lives with him, sleeps in a bed fit for a real queen, dines inside, in a kitchen, out of real dishes, plays with lots of toys, and gets brushed and petted daily.

# POCHINO'S FAMILY

In the summer of 2003, in the shadows of the city skyline, a litter of kittens was born in the far back corner of the alley behind our studio. These were the kittens that first captured our hearts because of their loyal commitment to one another, their unique functions within their family unit, and their extreme joy in simply being alive. It was there that Pochino, or Little Bit, a dainty, shy mama cat with exquisitely long, silky black hair, raised her four kittens. Papa came by occasionally in the early evenings, ostensibly to help stand watch, but this mama and her little ones generally fended for themselves.

Pochino quite obviously warned her children to beware of humans, even ones bearing food! For days all we saw were four sets of eyes, side by side, peeping out from underneath their dumpster home. It was this scene that first brought to our attention that homelessness, both human and animal, is a family affair.

They might have been cautious, but they were also curious! Finally, the bravest, a fluffy calico, ventured forth. One trip was all she needed, and she was in love — with the world. She looked around and was the queen of all she saw! We named her Christina, for her male counterpart Christopher Columbus. Like Columbus, Chris considered nothing beyond her realm of discovery and possibility.

Despite her mother's warnings, Chris feared nobody. In fact, she was very curious about the humans who brought the food. When she saw us, she strutted up to us as if she had known us for years. If we put our hands out toward her, she would come close enough to sniff our fingers. Her siblings obviously admired her spunk and

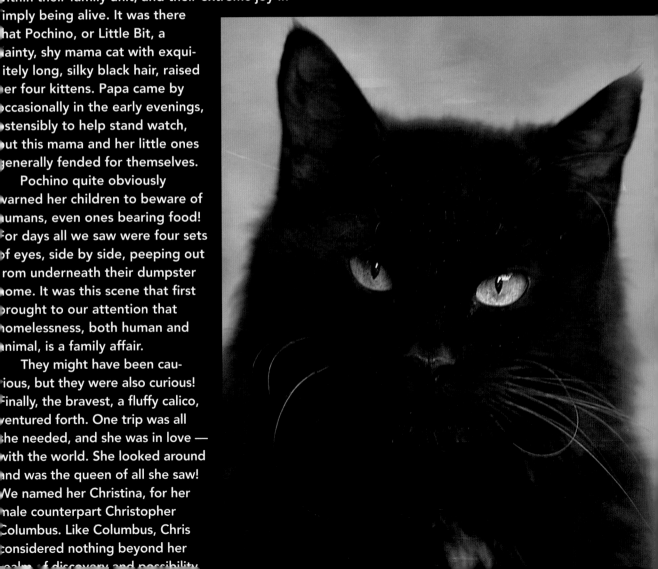

ventured out behind her, although they continued to hang back, somewhat in awe.

Boldly going where no alley cat had gone
before, Chris convinced her sisters and brother
to go to the very back of the alley in order to
play on a stack of pallets left outside one of
the businesses. There, the kittens, led by little
Chris, would jump on top, crawl underneath,
and weave in and out between pallets. They
were so small that they easily fit between the
boards. Chris performed her post-mealtime
ritual of bathing on the step of one of the
huge rigs in the alley. Of course, soon she
discovered many holes under the truck where
a kitten could play hide-and-seek. Again, she
persuaded her siblings to join in her game.
Like her distinctive markings, Chris's stride
was unique. She did not walk; she swaggered.
And everywhere she stopped to sit, she
perched very regally to survey her kingdom.

Sadly, one morning when the kittens were
about three months old, Chris did not appear.
We never saw her again. We had seen her the
evening before, and she was not ill. We
searched everywhere, calling out her name. We
have frequently wondered if, because of her
intrepid little nature, she was the first victim of
a coyote raid.

As the three remaining kittens aged, they
each became characters in their own right.
Tommaso, Tom for short, the single male, was
so named because he was indeed a Peeping
Tom. Tom never stepped daringly into the
open. Rather, he always peeped — from under
the tractor-trailer cab, behind a tire, between
pallets, around a storage shed, et cetera.

As he passed the peeping phase, Tom
became a complete clown. At first, he would
stand on two legs to bat at imaginary figments.
He played hide-and-seek with his sisters, with
rocks, with his tail, and with imaginary nothings
that could be seen only with his kitten's eyes.

Then nightly Tom began to choreograph and
perform the most intricate and energetic rou-
tines for his weary mom and incredulous sisters.
A large concrete slab at the back of the alley
served as his stage. The streetlights spot-
lighted his acts. He was a consummate actor,
able to portray distinct emotions and moods
with his eyes. At any given time, one could see
humor, disgust, melancholy, mischief, anger,
curiosity, or simple concentration in Tom's eyes.

The females were actually more aggressive
than their brother. Named for a Mafia enforcer,
Knuckles (a strange name for a girl, but a fitting
one for this particular female) came on duty at
mealtime. Establishing an imaginary border
around the food bowl, she patrolled it while
Tom and her sister Domino ate. Every night she
literally held four large gray cats at bay so her
family could eat their fill. Domenica, nicknamed
Domino, on the other hand, protected her
siblings more aggressively. A feisty little
fighter, Domino never hesitated to rush to
their aid. When she reached the site of the
conflict, she never slowed down but rather
ran straight into the melee, small white front
paws flying.

In fact, Domino was quite capable of
defending herself. One evening, Tom and
Domino began playing, but play soon esca-
lated to a serious altercation. Punches were
exchanged, but Tom found himself on the losing
side of this confrontation. As we watched,
Domino, a female feline Mohammad Ali, got
in six swipes to every one of Tom's.

Both girls also nurtured softer sides.
Despite her name and her mealtime role,
Knuckles preferred to remain close to home
and to mamma. Although beautiful, she rarely
groomed herself. As a result, her long fur constantly carried all manner of debris. Oblivious
and unconcerned, Knuckles rested near home
during the heat of the day, coming out only at

dusk. Her long hair made the heat unbearable for her. Her weary eyes reflected her misery. She found what little shade she could, usually under one of the big trucks in the alley or hidden beneath the brush at the alley's edge. When we searched for her, we could hear a rustling noise in the leaves and undergrowth. All we could see were her striking golden eyes gazing out at us.

Pochino's family of kittens was loyal and loving. We remained sure that the closeness of this little family was responsible for the fact that it flourished in spite of overwhelming odds. We took Tom, Domino, and Knuckles together to a loving home, where they continue to thrive. Although they are now part of a larger cat family, these three still love one another and act as one, not three, almost two years later. In the seventeenth century, the meta-physical poet John Donne said, "No man is an island." The same goes for cats, and these three have known this simple lesson since birth.

# POSSUM'S GANG

**P**ossum's Gang was like a human street gang — scrappy, enduring, street-smart, and battle-scarred. The gang members were the remaining cats from two litters of kittens born in the heat of the summer of 2003. Their mothers had themselves been littermates just the summer before and had lived in the alley without much notice. Skittish and bland, they simply skulked about. Spitter, Possum's mother, gave birth to her kittens beneath a dumpster in the alley, while her sister Spooner gave birth to hers in a partial burrow on the edge of the alley in a thicket of trees and bushes. Thus previously nondescript cats became attentive, caring parents.

Virtually from birth, Possum claimed leadership of her gang. The first time we saw her, she was only days old. In fact, she could barely stand up for more than seconds at a time. She was solid gray with a white stripe down her face. Other than a few meager strands of hair on her head, her body was so void of hair that she looked like a hairless breed. In fact, she looked exactly like a possum; hence, her name.

Possum's soul mate from birth was as beautiful as Possum was unattractive. We named her Queenie. Even at an early stage of development, she was a glittering shade of absolute silver perfection. Possum and Queenie formed a relationship from birth that was to last their entire short lives, for they were always together. They literally lived in each other's shadow. Other gang members were Tiger, a beautiful caramel tabby with jaguar spots; Face, a handsome, deep-gray male so named because of a facial parasite that completely changed the contour of his face; and Little Gal, a beautiful silver female like Queenie but with faint patches of caramel throughout her coat. Certainly the least attractive and the smallest, Possum was nevertheless the undisputed leader of the gang. The others watched her for unspoken permission. Even when she gave her tacit approval, they often would only look on in wonder and longing, for they were not brave enough to tackle the task.

Meanwhile, the other litter of kittens, although born first, was never as visible. There was a fluffy white kitten that we named Ytee. The only other kitten from that litter that we know of was a dark-gray kitten with that conspicuous white stripe down the bridge of her nose that also marked Possum, but with the biggest ears on the smallest head imaginable! She had long, gangly legs and was absurd to watch. She looked like a donkey, and that became her name.

These two litters combined forces and wits after a life-and-death struggle with a coyote. When Donkey was less than six weeks old, the stillness of the night was shattered by a piercing, blood-curdling scream. The shrieks continued and were combined with guttural growling noises, sounds of bones crunching, and the smacking sound as one body in the jaws of another was whipped back and forth. A city coyote attacked late one evening. Ytee was the first to be taken. And Ytee's dad, a large gray tabby named Razor, was also killed as he tried valiantly to defend his family. He was no small cat, and it was his howls that splintered the night. The surviving mother and Donkey, her one remaining kitten, joined her sister's litter under the dumpster. The gray father of Possum's gang assumed protection of these two additions. As Donkey became integrated into his cousins' litter, she was definitely the outsider. First, being about three weeks older, she was significantly larger than the other kittens. Second, she still closely resembled her namesake, which made her a little ugly. However, most notably, she was so wary and jumpy that if she had been a person, she would have been called crazy or, at the very least, hyperactive. Intuitively, we knew that her behavior had to do with what she had seen and endured the night her family and father had been killed. Donkey seemed to us a clear example of PTSD (post-traumatic stress disorder) in cats.

The coyotes were not the only enemies that Possum's Gang had to fight, but they were the most violent. They were also an ever-present threat. Early one evening just a few weeks after the death of Donkey's family, a coyote killed Queenie. After the death of her soul mate, Possum seemed very much alone. For several days she remained aloof from the others. She did not look for Queenie; she seemed intuitively to know what had happened. Their mother carried her sorrow as well; in fact, the day after the deaths, she paced and wailed loud, long, low mournful cries. She could not settle down and would have nothing to do with the other cats and kittens. Eventually, her daily worries about survival and caring for the kittens as well as her sibling's litter seemed to calm the turmoil in her mind.

Each evening the female cats would place themselves strategically in the alley for night watch. One mother would sit high on a wall overlooking the alley, while the other one perched on a large metal post. From their elevated positions, they could see everything.

When the father cat was present, he placed himself between his kittens and the top of the alley. They fought with raccoons for food every night. Although the raccoons were not directly harmful to Possum's Gang, they were vultures, devouring food left out for the cats and destroying food and water bowls. The raccoons also carried diseases. One afternoon a raccoon wandered near the food bowls. Clearly he was suffering, for he could neither stand nor walk straight. His right side seemed partially paralyzed. His mouth hung open, and he was completely unafraid either of the mother cats who steadfastly defended their kittens' food or of us. Even we were wary of him. At that point, we decided to trap the raccoons and remove them to a lake area far from the city and Possum's Gang.

There were good times for Possum and her gang. In the early evenings, when the sun sank just low enough that it was no longer beating directly down on the alley and its inhabitants, the kittens would come from their various hiding places and gather to eat. With their tummies full, they would play until they were exhausted. Their first exposure to commercial toys terrified them; they preferred natural toys, such as dried leaves, twigs, and sections of string. One evening they entertained themselves batting around an empty bullet shell they had found. Just as they let us bring them food, they gradually let us play with them from the other end of a rope or a stick. We like to think that these evenings were as peaceful for Possum and her family as they were for us.

As one might expect, the worst enemy for Possum's Gang, even unintentionally, was humans. Living in an alley does not protect animals (or people, for that matter) from cars. Actually, the cars are only the instruments of injury and death; the drivers are the ones wielding these machines, usually carelessly but

sometimes, sadly, intentionally. One drizzly morning, a car speeding to work down the alley hit little Possum. Grievously, it did not kill her immediately. We rushed her to the vet, who diagnosed a broken pelvis at the very minimum. Not wanting to subject Possum to any further pain or fear, we refused X-rays to check for internal injuries. Possum received fluids and pain medicine, and the vet put her in intensive care. The vet assured us that Possum would not suffer; in fact, if there were no internal injuries, she might even survive. She lived through the day and into the late evening. But sometime during the night, she died. We were devastated and carried such guilt for not having had her immediately euthanized. Our instincts had told us that she could not last, but we allowed our hope to dictate our actions and little Possum's final hours. Although she was in shock, she nonetheless seemed to trust her fate to us. We had forgotten that our abiding obligation was to safeguard her, rather than our own feelings.

The remaining members of Possum's original gang continued to live in the alley throughout the winter. However, they never recovered from their losses, almost as if they had been forced into adulthood prematurely. The death of Donkey's mom from a respiratory illness only emphasized their sadness. Gradually, all of them — Tiger, Little Gal, Face, and even Donkey — became accustomed to human touch. What began as quick pats while they were eating grew gradually, through real trust, into much more. Tiger showed her true stripes. The gentlest of the little cats, she was, in reality, no tiger at all, but a true lap cat. She would sit for hours to feel human hands stroking her fur. Face preferred the belly rub. No sooner would he spot us than he would flop down on his side and expose his tender underbelly for us to rub. And, possibly the sweetest story of all, Donkey

calmed during the winter and became a true companion to Face, Tiger, and Little Gal. She, too, wanted human contact and absolutely loved to have the area just above her tail scratched. In fact, our scratches were met by the quickest, most incredibly strong butt-raising response we have seen in a cat!

During the winter the four young cats were almost constantly together. At night they slept together in one large ball on a fluffy comforter in a cat house we had built for them several months earlier. During daylight, if the four cats separated, Face and Donkey explored as a team; they became close companions. Tiger would appear with the boys early in the morning but remained nearby when they left. On the other hand, Little Gal consistently slept late after being the last to bed the previous night; she never arose before 10 AM. Face emerged as the leader of this smaller gang, for he was obviously both the hunter/gatherer and the protector.

Early one morning just as spring began, the unthinkable happened. Face left the relative safety of his alley to cross the road to hunt. When he was returning home, a car struck and killed him instantly. In less than a second, a

feral kitten that had survived severe illness, adjusted to permanent facial paralysis, suffered the loss of family members, learned to trust selected human friends, and grown into a responsible, loving young cat, was gone. We buried Face and sobbed that we would never see him grow into adulthood. Tiger, Little Gal, and especially Donkey seemed lost and adrift without their buddy and his strength.

As alley cats know too well, life goes on. So, too, does Possum's Gang, down to only three members. We feel blessed to know and have known all the original members of Possum's Gang. Of the survivors, Tiger never gives up hope of life beyond the alley. Little Gal demonstrates the value of play in our lives. Donkey provides us with a living example of courage and faith that life can get better. Even those who have gone fill us with eternal hope. Queenie offers us hope that there is a soul mate for each of us. Face, a serious-looking alley cat who loved belly rubs, teaches us daily what trust is. Possum, a little feral kitten and leader of the gang, remains in our hearts as the epitome of true exuberance and self-confidence despite all odds.

# EPILOGUE

Remember when we demonstrated how many kittens can come from just one unspayed female? Well, we have living proof! Unfortunately, we overlooked a single female in our quest to spay all females. It turned out to be Spitter, a gray female and the mother of the ill-fated litter to which Possum belonged.

As a result, in the early summer of 2004, four new kittens came down the hill from the office buildings next door to the food and water bowls set up in our alley. There were two beautiful calicos, white with big splotches of orange, black, and brown, and two striking tabbies. Because of the amount of orange in their coats, we knew immediately that Nemesis, too shrewd to be trapped, was the father. We named the calicos Lucy (for another redhead) and Shiner, for the circle of black around her left eye. The little female tabby

we named Olive, while the male became Roscoe.

A coyote almost got Lucy late one night, but she fought fearlessly and escaped his clutches. However, the coyote probably broke the tiny bones in her right front paw and left a huge puncture wound in the right side of her neck. We tried unsuccessfully to catch her and take her to the vet, but she hid from us and from her family. When she finally emerged, she was walking on only three legs, and the wound on her neck remained open. Very wary still, she persisted in running from us. Gradually, she healed, although on cold mornings, even months later, she still limped. As she began to trust us again, we managed to capture her for spaying and returned her to her colony in the alley, where she flourished. One cool morning, Lucy did not appear for her breakfast. We searched for her throughout the day before we found her body lifeless behind a trailer. We could find no marks on her. She was clearly the victim of foul play. Our hearts broke as we realized she survived a coyote's jaw only to be killed by a human.

Shiner and Olive were so very friendly from the outset that it was fairly easy to find them homes just before Christmas 2004. Roscoe, the only male in the litter, and a little devil, evidently bothered a larger cat one too many times and was slapped between the eyes with a claw. Subsequently, he developed a huge abscess. We grabbed him and took him to the vet, where he was neutered and his abscess treated. As with his other siblings, he was such a sweetie that we easily found him a home, where he is now a spoiled rotten top cat in the making.

Following this first litter, Spitter again gave birth to three more kittens in late October 2004. Once more, Nemesis sired kittens stamped with his vivid orange markings and widely set light-ginger eyes. The only female, another calico whom we named Cali Rose, aka Rosie, is probably the sweetest kitten to come from the alley. She is now spayed and comfortably ensconced in her very own home. The two

little males were Frankie, a gorgeous black-and-white version of Nemesis, and Shakes, a tabby.

Spitter was spayed and returned to the alley, where she became a favorite of Knox, because of her fiery personality. One day while Knox was searching for her, he came across her skeleton, again seemingly a victim of human cruelty. Frankie died soon after and Shakes was run over by a truck.

As for the fate of the other cats that came from our alley, Tom, Domino, Knuckles, and Tiger all have loving homes. Kat remains with the Protector. We rereleased Pochino, Donkey, Little Gal, and Muncher (an infrequent gray tabby visitor who wandered into our trap) into the alley following their neutering and vaccinations. Thankfully, none of the cats from our alley tested positive for feline leukemia or feline AIDS. We feed everyone daily, and they recognize us as good friends now. One day we fully expect one of the cats to knock on our office door, wanting us to come out to play or asking why dinner is late.

Possum was cremated and her ashes scattered. Face is buried in a pretty spot by one of the buildings next to the alley alongside Lucy, Shakes, and many others.

# LASTING IMAGES

We are not cat experts; rather, we are cat (and all animal) lovers. We believe facts are important. However, facts alone do not always communicate the entire picture. Sometimes they fail to truly express the despair, the urgency, the reality, or the joy that exists in a situation. These are the things we hope our photographs and stories have conveyed to you. In completing our cat stories, we want to share with you a few lasting images that will forever be seared in our memories.

Our last view of Razor, a beautiful, daunting gray tomcat and father, sitting erect and imposing in the middle of the alley, watching as his kittens played and his mate slept.

twice its normal size, his little ears burning with fever, so sick he could barely move, from a parasite transmitted by a fly.

Spooner, Donkey's mom, the two of them the sole survivors of the coyote attack, her mouth open, her eyes swollen with grief.

Opening the studio door one summer's night to find little Face, sitting on his rear haunches on the landing outside the door, looking up expectantly.

Only weeks later, little Face's flattened, unrecognizable body on the road in front of our studio. We identified him only by the color of his fur and his white foot.

Nemesis then and now. Then, a powerful,

male. Now, less than three years later, a gaunt, hollow-eyed, scraggly tomcat.

Tiger, not weighing yet two pounds, growling as if she weighed ninety pounds, clawing and scratching every exposed inch of my skin, jumping from my arms, and high tailing it down the alley to safety, after I rescued her from a storage shed.

Brave, stoic Lucy walking for days on three legs after escaping a coyote's clutches.

Frankie and Rosie, two new little kittens, perched up in their "eagle's nest" in a tree, watching their world go by.

Spooner, hacking with a cough, huddled in a blanket we put out for her under the streetlight.

Little Gal, calling to her buddy Knox in her soft, high-pitched squeak from her nightly vigil on the roof of the office building.

Queenie and Possum, always sleeping curled up in one another. We trust they will be together that way forever.

We are fortunate to have spent the last two-and-a-half years participating in our own Trap-Neuter-Return (TNR) program. The surviving cats who remain in our colony have changed as a result of our association, just as we have. We think they would agree with us that the effort has been mutually beneficial. Most certainly as a result of our observations and our work, we have come to view as supreme arrogance the human view that we are the only species worth the struggle to protect and aid.

## ABOUT THE AUTHORS

KNOX is an acclaimed photographer, known for his dramatic, gritty, and realistic visual take on street life. He has also worked in the music business for the last thirty years in New York City and Atlanta, where he is now based. His websites are www.urbantailsbook.com and www.avatarphotoart.com.

SARA NEELEY, a freelance writer, has spent her entire life writing and teaching others to write. A former English teacher, she has a master's degree in English literature.

## ABOUT THE PUBLISHER

NEW WORLD LIBRARY is dedicated to publishing books and other media that inspire and challenge us to improve the quality of our lives and the world.

Our products are available in bookstores everywhere. For our catalog, please contact:

New World Library
14 Pamaron Way
Novato, California 94949

Phone: 415-884-2100 or 800-972-6657
Catalog requests: Ext. 50
Orders: Ext. 52
Fax: 415-884-2199
Email: escort@newworldlibrary.com
Website: www.newworldlibrary.com

TO LEARN HOW YOU CAN HELP
visit our website, www.urbantailsbook.com